LORD JIM

Borgo Press Dramas by FRANK J. MORLOCK

Chuzzlewit
Crime and Punishment
Falstaff (with William Shakespeare, John Dennis, and William Kendrick)
Fathers and Sons
The Idiot
Justine
Lord Jim
The Marquis de Sade (with Charles Méré)
Notes from the Underground
Oblomov
Outrageous Women: Lady Macbeth and Other French Plays (editor and translator)
Peter and Alexis
The Princess Casamassima
A Raw Youth
The Stendhal Hamlet Scenarios and Other Shakespearean Shorts from the French (editor and translator)

LORD JIM
A PLAY IN TWO ACTS

FRANK J. MORLOCK

Adapted from the Novel by Joseph Conrad

THE BORGO PRESS
MMXII

LORD JIM

Copyright © 1965, 2012 by Frank J. Morlock

FIRST BORGO PRESS EDITION

Published by Wildside Press LLC

www.wildsidebooks.com

DEDICATION

For James Ludlum

CONTENTS

CAST OF CHARACTERS 9
ACT I 13
ACT II 83
ABOUT THE AUTHOR 141

CAST OF CHARACTERS

Marlow

1st Guest

2nd Guest

3rd Guest

Examiner

Jim

Captain

Engineer

First Mate

Judge/Brierly

Lafarge

Bailiff

One of the Spectators

Another Spectator

Stein

Doramin

Cornelius

Tam iTam

Brown

A Yankee

Jewel

Natives, Spectators at the Inquest

LORD JIM

ACT I

Marlow is seated with his friends at a table on the audience's left. To the right of the stage is a dais for the three judges and a witness booth. There are seats for the spectators. Where Marlow is, however, there is a suggestion of a balcony and palm trees. Marlow is a man in his mid–fifties. When he talks about the past he gets up and walks across the stage to the courtroom and sits as a spectator. The courtroom area remains dark until Marlow walks into it. When he does walk into it, the balcony area becomes dark.

Marlow (to his friend)

It was a truly strange case.

Guest

Tell us.

Marlow

It happened this way.

(Marlow rises and moves into the courtroom.)

Examiner

Do you know where the other officers of the *Patna* may be?

Jim

The engineer is dead.

Examiner

I know that. I was referring to the others.

Jim

No.

Examiner

They are summoned to appear or forfeit their licenses. Do you know why they might not wish to testify?

Jim

That's obvious, isn't it?

Examiner

This is not a criminal prosecution.

Jim

Still, it is a disgrace.

Examiner

Then, why are you here? It's embarrassing for you, too, isn't it?

Jim

Yes, but I must see it through.

Examiner

I want you to realize that I am only here to get the truth. I have no vendetta against anyone. I have no preconceptions. This is only a hearing to determine if the officers' licenses should be cancelled. You understand that?

Jim

Yes.

Examiner

I want you to think of me as your friend, not your enemy. May I call you by your first name?

Jim

I don't object.

Examiner

Jim, is it? Were you the first mate, Jim?

Jim

No, I was the second mate.

Examiner

Now, will you tell us what happened on the *Patna* the night of the disaster.

Jim

I was standing third watch. The rest of the crew was asleep or off duty except for the Lascars. We were running smoothly over a calm sea.

Examiner

One moment. There were passengers on your ship?

Jim

Yes.

Examiner

How many?

Jim

Roughly eight hundred Indian Muslims making a pilgrimage to Mecca.

Examiner

That was just to set the record straight. Go ahead with your story.

Jim

Well, a short time later, we hit something. Whatever it was, it pealed a good deal of the hull right off, just like the skin off a tangerine.

Examiner

Where was the captain, Jim?

Jim

The captain was arguing with the engineer. The captain was in his underwear. They had both been drinking.

Examiner

What was the argument about?

Jim

The captain was a German.

Examiner

We know that. Just tell us what brought on the argument.

Jim

It was a drunken squabble.

(Enter the captain and the engineer on the raised part of the stage.)

Captain

Where did you get that drink?

Engineer

Drink? Not from you, captain, that's for sure. You're far too stingy. You'd sooner see a man dead than spare him a drop of your precious schnapps. That's what you Germans call economy. Penny wise; pound foolish. (shouting) I only had one. So help me!

Captain

You're drunk, *du schwein*.

Engineer (drunkenly)

Who's drunk? Me! Oh no, no, captain, that won't do. Not on your rations. I've never been drunk in my life. Nothing comes out of a bottle that can make me drunk! I can drink you and the rest of the crew under the table and still be sober. If I thought I was drunk, you know what I'd do? I'd jump overboard. You know why? Because I don't like you any better than those dirty little niggers.

Captain

You deserve a good sound beating.

Engineer

I'm not afraid of you. It's a good thing for you that there are people in this world who are afraid of their own shadows. Where would you be if these—

(The captain pushes the engineer, calling him "*schwein*." There is a sudden crashing thud. Suddenly the captain and the engineer fade out and we are with Jim again on the main platform.)

Examiner

So you concluded then that you had collided with something afloat. What was it? A waterlogged wreck?

Jim

I don't know.

Examiner

Did your captain give you any orders?

Jim

Yes. He said to call us one by one and make no noise for fear of creating a panic among the passengers. I thought it was a very reasonable precaution.

Examiner

Yes. I'm sure you thought so.

Jim

I took one of the lamps that hung under the awnings and went forward. I climbed down the foredeck and saw it was more than half full of water already. I knew there must be a big hole somewhere below the waterline

Examiner

Yes, yes. So, you knew there was a hole? Then what did you do? Were you afraid, Jim?

Jim (loudly)

No. No. I wasn't afraid. (pause) I didn't even think of danger. I might have been startled, that's all. All this happened so quickly. And then, everything was so quiet.

Examiner

Go on.

Jim

I knew there was no other bulkhead, but the collision separating the forepack from the forehold.

Examiner

Try to tell me step by step.

Jim

Before I got there, I met the engineer at the foot of the bridge ladder. He was dazed. He said he had slipped on the ladder and broken his left arm. He was afraid the bulkhead would give way and that we would sink immediately. I didn't have much better hope. He told me the ship was unseaworthy. Then he shoved by me and ran back up the ladder shouting to the captain. I followed him. The captain knocked him flat on his face. He only hit him once. Then he hissed at him: "Get up. Block the skylight." The engineer cursed and did as he was told.

Examiner

What was the purpose of this?

Jim

The engine room connected with the passenger deck. If the skylight was blocked they couldn't reach the bridge except by the main ladder.

Examiner

You mean, then, that there was an attempt to imprison the passengers?

Jim

Yes.

Examiner

Wasn't that pretty close to attempted murder? How many passengers were there again?

Jim

Eight hundred.

Examiner

And how many lifeboats?

Jim

Seven. Not enough. Not nearly enough. The ship was not prepared for an emergency.

Examiner

Was it then that the lifeboats were loosed?

Jim

I was coming to that. No, it wasn't then. I went back to the bulkhead. The captain ordered me to look again. I think now that he wanted me out of the way. But it didn't occur to me then.

Examiner

Oh, I see. It didn't occur to you then what he had in mind. Very well. You went back?

Jim

Yes. The bulkhead was bulging! Bulging, I tell you. And there was steam escaping from the pipes. I didn't think that anything could be done. I expected it to go momentarily. I was sure we were going to sink.

Examiner

And what did you do?

Jim

For a while I just stood there staring. What was there to do but wait? The boats couldn't carry even a hundred. No, not even jammed. If I had roused the passengers, assuming there was time to do it, the panic might have taken any chance we had. We don't know how to handle these natives in an emergency. They're quite strange.

Examiner

Yes, yes. That's quite so, quite so. Now, you did not at that moment loose the lifeboats?

Jim

No, I went back on deck.

Examiner

Why didn't you warn them then?

Judge

Just one moment. I don't think that you need to answer that question.

Jim

I don't object to answering the question.

Examiner

This is not a criminal prosecution.

Judge

It might lead to a criminal prosecution. I advise you of your right not to answer the question.

Jim

I wish to answer the question. I didn't know what to do. The situation was such that any effort we could have made would have been useless.

Examiner

But there were no efforts made, were there? You're sure you weren't afraid?

Jim

No. I am ready to swear I was not afraid.

Examiner

I didn't ask you that. What did you do, since you weren't afraid?

Jim

I went back to see the captain. I had to go through the passenger section. They were asleep. Stepping over one sleeping fellow, I accidentally roused him. He clung to me.

Examiner

And?

Jim

I fought him off. I had to knock him out.

Examiner

You had to knock him out?

Jim

Yes. He was sick. He wanted water. I couldn't get free of him. He had hold of my leg. I had to hit him.

Examiner

And, you were never afraid all this time? Not once?

Jim

No, I was not afraid.

Examiner

Of course you weren't.

Jim

I was trying to get to the boats; I was going to free them. That was my only thought.

Examiner

So, you decided to save the lives of some at least.

Jim

Yes, some of the passengers' lives.

Examiner

All right. Go on.

Jim

As I was clinging to the bridge, the engineer tried to hit me with a monkey wrench. I was going to hit him, but he said he thought I was one of the niggers. The captain was busy about one of the boats. He shouted to me and then came charging at me. I wasn't afraid of him. I just stood there and was ready to defend myself.

Examiner

You seem to have been engaged in quite a bit of—

Jim

All he said was: "Oh, it's you. Lend a hand." I was ready enough until I knew what it was I was to help with. I asked him if he was going to do it. He said: "Yes, clear out." I really don't think I understood him at first.

Examiner

No doubt his English was poor.

Jim

I was nearly out of my mind with worry.

Examiner

What was your reaction?

Jim

I did nothing. I didn't move. I didn't speak. I just looked. The ship was beginning to list slightly. I thought perhaps we might shore up the bulkhead. But it seemed useless, so I stood there, staring.

Examiner

In other words, you froze?

Jim

I wouldn't put it that way. I just didn't know what to do. Then, finally....

Examiner

You decided to pitch in?

Jim

No, I didn't. The engineer and the captain were trying to launch a lifeboat. They weren't able to work together. They were both terrified. The captain called me to help.

(Silence. The captain appears on the upper stage again.)

Captain

Come and help, man! Are you mad to throw away your only chance? Come and help! Why don't you come, you miserable coward? If I had time, I'd crack your skull for you. Won't you save your own life?

Jim

He called me a coward. Isn't that funny?

(Silence.)

Jim (to the court)

I saw a squall rising behind us. Big, black. Black! Black! And I knew we were all going to die.

Engineer (screaming at Jim)

Why don't you help? You, you're the biggest. You're the strongest. Why don't you help us?

Jim

Suddenly I rushed under the boat and cut it free. Then I cut all the other boats free. I did this as fast as I could.

Engineer

You silly fool. Do you think those niggers will give you a chance? They'll kill us all.

Examiner

So, you helped them after all?

Jim

No. I did the only thing there was to do. I loosed the boats. Then I waited.

Examiner

What did you wait for?

Jim

I don't know.

Examiner

So you did nothing?

Jim (flatly)

I did nothing.

Examiner

Meanwhile, the captain and the first mate managed to launch the boat. And you still hadn't made up your mind to go with them?

Jim

No. I kept apart. I tried to maintain a certain distance from the others. I couldn't stop them all from what they were doing, but I had no intention of participating in it. It was a shameful thing to do.

Examiner

Then, why is it, can you explain, that you wound up in

that little boat?

(The captain appears again.)

Captain

Shove! Shove for your life. The squall will be on us in a second.

Jim (turns to the court)

I decided to walk back to the passenger deck. I don't know what my purpose was. I stumbled over the legs of the engineer. He must have fallen.

(The captain and first mate come onto the second level. They are now in the lifeboat.)

Jim

They called to the engineer. In the dark, they took me for him.

First Mate

George, Jamy.

Captain

The squall, *mein Gott*!

First Mate

Shove off. We can't wait any longer. She's going down.

Jim

And I jumped.

Judge

You may step down.

Examiner

I call as the next witness Lieutenant Lafarge of the *Victorieuse*. (Lafarge goes to the stand) Would you please identify yourself?

Lafarge

I am Lieutenant Armand Lafarge of the *Victorieuse*. She is a gunboat. A very pretty little craft. Very pretty. Tres coquette.

Examiner

Would you tell us what happened on the morning after the events described by the last witness?

Lafarge

Oui, monsieur. At about 0900 hours we were bound for

Réunion. We sighted the *Patna* floating dangerously by the head.

Examiner

How did you know anything was wrong?

Lafarge

There was an ensign union down flying from her main gaff. The sarang had apparently the sense to signal distress. When we got closer we saw the decks were packed like a sheep pen. There were Indians jammed along the bridge and rails in a solid mass. Hundreds of eyes stared at us and yet not a sound was made. We hailed, but got no intelligible reply.

Examiner

Did you board immediately?

Lafarge

No, *monsieur*. We, afraid of plague, looked them over for some time through binoculars. The captain decided to send a boat.

Examiner

You were on the boarding party?

Lafarge

I was sent aboard. We found out little from the sarang and tried to talk to an Arab. But we couldn't make head or tail out of it.

Examiner

You didn't understand?

Lafarge

It was the absence of a crew that startled us. Of course, the nature of the emergency was obvious. We were also very struck by the dead body of a white man lying on the bridge. In fact, *fort intrigue par cette cadavre.*

Examiner

And there were no white officers aboard the ship?

Lafarge

No, *monsieur. Impossible de comprend se vous concevez.*

Judge

Will you please speak in English?

Lafarge

Oh, *pardon, monsieur.* We just didn't understand. The passengers crowded around the dead man.

Examiner

Did you examine the body, Lieutenant Lafarge?

Lafarge

One had to attend to the most pressing problems. There people were beginning to agitate themselves. *Parbleu*, a mob like that you don't see.

Examiner

Back to the body. Was death natural, Lafarge?

Lafarge

Oui, monsieur. It appeared to be a heart attack.

Examiner

What then?

Lafarge

I checked the bulkhead. I advised my captain that the safest thing to do was to leave it alone. It was a villainous thing.

Examiner

And you managed to save the ship?

Lafarge

We got two hawsers aboard and took the *Patna* in tow. That bulkhead demanded the greatest care. The greatest care. We pulled it stern foremost because the rudder was too much out of the water to be of any use for steering. This maneuver eased the strain on the bulkhead. Luckily the sea was calm. And there was no wind.

Examiner

What did you do then?

Lafarge

Why, we took the *Patna* to the nearest port, naturalmente, where the responsibility ceased, *dieu merci*. Mind you, all the time we were towing we had two men stationed at the tow lines to cut the ship free in the event that.... (he gestures)

Examiner

You remained aboard, however?

Lafarge

I was aboard that *Patna* with two men for thirty hours. That miserable *Patna*. I think it was unworthy to dignify by the name of ship. Thirty hours!

Examiner

Was the ship seaworthy, in your opinion before the mishap?

Lafarge

No. It was judged proper that one of our officers should remain and keep an eye open and communicate by signals with *Victorieuse*, do you see. We took measures. It was a delicate position and no wine, *monsieur*. For thirty hours. Not a drop. And for me, you know, when it comes to eating without my wine, I am nowhere. (gestures again, laughter) But we reached port without an incident.

Examiner

At the port, everyone behaved quite calmly?

Lafarge

One might have thought they had such a droll find brought to them every day. It was curious, that dead man.

Examiner

And there were living men, too? Much more curious.

Lafarge

The devil, bah! Very interesting, that is it. That is it

Examiner

What are you referring to?

Lafarge

That young man who just testified, who got himself mixed up with those others. After all, one does not die of it.

Examiner

Die of what?

Lafarge

Of being afraid. One is always afraid, *monsieur*. Always one may talk, but the fear, the fear, look you, is always there. (he slaps his chest like Jim) Yes, *monsieur*. One talks, one talks. But in the end, one is no cleverer than the next man and no more brave. Brave, this is always to be seen. I have rolled my hump in all corners of the world. I have known famous men, brave men. Brave, *vous concevez*. In the service, one has got to be. The trade demands it. Well, *eh bien*, each of them, I say, each of them. If he were an honest man, *bien entendu*, would admit, there is a point where you let go everything. You have got to live with that truth, do you see? Given a certain combination of circumstances, the fear is sure to come. Abominable, but true. And even for those who do not believe this truth, there is fear also. The fear of themselves. Absolutely so, sir, trust me. Trust me. Take me, for instance. I have had my proofs. *Eh bien*, I who am speaking to you. No, no, one does not die of it.

Examiner

You think cowardice is natural to man?

Lafarge

That is so, *monsieur*. Man is born a coward. It is difficult. It would be easy otherwise. The example of others, one puts up with it. And the fact that others are no better than yourself. That young man, you will observe, had all of these inducements. We may have had the best dispositions, the very best dispositions.

Examiner

I am glad to see someone takes a lenient view.

Lafarge

Pardon, allow me. I continued that one may get on

very well knowing that one's courage does not come of itself. One truth the more ought not to make life impossible. There is nothing much in that. But the honor. The honor, *monsieur*. That is real. And what life may be worth, when the honor is gone, ah, *par example*, I can offer no opinion, because I know nothing of it, *monsieur*. I do not think of it.

Examiner

It is good that you do not have to. Thank you very much, lieutenant. You may step down.

Judge

This inquiry is adjourned until tomorrow at eleven. You may rise.

Bailiff

All stand.

(Judges rise. One Judge approaches Marlow.)

One of the Spectators

You know that was a strange thing. Not being able to see the ship. No lights.

Another Spectator

But, of course, he would lie.

Brierly (walking up to Marlow)

Ah, Marlow, you here.

Marlow

I didn't expect to see you as judge, Brierly.

Brierly

They caught me for it, you see. Very inconvenient for me and God knows how long it will last. Three days, I suppose.

Marlow

Rotten, isn't it?

Brierly

Gad, what's the use of it? It's the stupidest thing imaginable. It makes me feel a fool.

Marlow

What option is there?

Brierly

Why do we have to torment that boy?

Marlow

I don't know. Unless it's that he lets you.

Brierly

I suppose that's it. Can't he see that dirty captain of his has cleared out. Nothing can save the boy. He'll lose his license. He's damned lucky no prosecution will follow. But he's all washed up as a seaman. Why eat all that crap?

Marlow

Well, we know that that captain has feathered his nest pretty well. He can procure almost any means of getting away. With this fellow Jim it's not such an easy matter. The government's keeping him in the sailors' home for the time being and he probably hasn't the money to run. It costs money to run away.

Brierly

Does it? Not always. (laughs) Well then, why doesn't he just dig a hole for himself and stay there? He could, for all I care.

Marlow

You must give him credit for a kind of courage in facing it out, knowing that he could run away and no one would bother to run after him.

Brierly

Courage be damned! That sort of courage is of no use to keep a man straight. I don't give a damn for courage like that. If you were to say it is a kind of cowardice, of softness, ah, I tell you what! I'll put up two hundred rupees if you'll put up another hundred and undertake to make that beggar clear out tonight, before he takes the stand again.

Marlow

The fellow's a gentleman.

Brierly

If he is, he'll understand. He must. The publicity is too shocking. He sits there with all these confounded natives, lascars, Frenchies, Hindus and God knows what kind of aborigines looking on and gives evidence that's enough to burn a man to ashes with shame. It's abominable. Why, Marlow, don't you see, don't you feel this is an abomination? Now, come, as a seaman, don't you? If he went away all this would stop at once. The inquiry would be closed and all this would be over with.

Marlow

And what does the cowardice of all these men matter, really? They're just four men.

Brierly

And you call yourself a seaman, I suppose?

Marlow

That's what I call myself, and I hope I am one, too.

Brierly

Balls! You have no sense of dignity. You don't think enough of what you are supposed to be.

Marlow

And, what are we supposed to be?

Brierly

Men. It's a disgrace. We've got all kinds among us. Some scoundrels, yes. But damn it, we've got to preserve our professional dignity, or we're no better than a gang of pirates. We are trusted. Don't you understand? Trusted. Frankly, I don't care a damn for all those Hindus on that boat. But a decent man would not have behaved like this to a cargo of rags and bales. We aren't an organized body of men, and the only thing that holds us together is just our name and reputation for dignity and decency. Pride. An affair like this destroys confidence that people have in us. What's worse, it destroys our confidence in ourselves. You may go through your entire life on the sea with no occasion to show your stuff, but if the time comes, and you don't, if.... (breaks off) I'll give you two hundred rupees, Marlow. You just talk that chap into leaving. Fact is, I think my family actually knows his. His father's a parson; yes, in fact, I've met him. It's horrible. I can't do it myself, but if you...ah...

Marlow

I'm not going to meddle in this. I don't know what you take me for. I'm not a bag man, or whatever you may think I am.

Brierly

Oh well, forget it. I suppose you're right.

(They begin to leave the courtroom. A dog is noticeable in the doorway frame.)

Marlow

Watch out for that cur.

(Brierly and Marlow separate.)

Brierly

I suppose you'll be here tomorrow?

Marlow

Yes, I think so.

Brierly

Well, till then.

Jim (evenly but menacingly)

Did you speak to me, sir?

Marlow

No.

Jim

You say no. But I heard.

Marlow

There must be some mistake. As far as I know, I haven't opened my mouth in front of you.

Jim

What did you mean by staring at me all this morning?

Marlow

Did you expect everyone to bow his head out of respect for your feelings?

Jim

No, that's all right. Only, only, I won't let any man call me names outside this court. There was someone with you.

Marlow

Yes. The chief judge. Captain Brierly.

Jim

You spoke to him. Yes, I know it's all very fine. You spoke to him. But you meant me to hear.

Marlow

I assure you, you are mistaken. I have no idea how you could fancy I was speaking of you.

Jim

You thought I would be afraid to resent this. If you were twice your size I would tell you what I think of you. You....

Marlow

Stop. Now, just what am I supposed to have said? Tell me.

Jim

I will show you that I am not.

Marlow

What the hell are you talking about? You don't make sense.

Jim

Now that you see I am not afraid, you try to weasel out of it. Who's a cur now, eh? I will allow no man....

Marlow

You don't think I was talking about you, do you?

Jim

I am sure I heard....

Marlow

Don't be a fool. Look.

Jim

But, I heard....

Marlow

Look.

(Jim sees the dog.)

Jim

Oh God! (voice breaking) I'm sorry. My mistake entirely. You'll forgive me.

(Jim starts to rush away.)

Marlow

Don't go like that.

Jim

You understand. All these people staring at me, I'm very sorry. I'm sure that others have been saying it or thinking it. And, and I just can't put up with it. And I don't intend to. In court it's different. I've got to stand that. I will do it.

Marlow

Now look, why don't you come and have a drink with me at my hotel?

Jim

Thank you. But....

Marlow

I insist.

(Marlow leaves Jim and walks to the table at the audience's left and sits with his friends.)

Marlow

Ah. And so, you see that's how it was, how I met him. And then I invited him to my club! And we talked for a while and he told me his story.

(The stage darkens completely. When the lights go up the guests are gone and Marlow and Jim are together. The guests are walking in the background of the veranda.)

Jim

It's very kind of you to listen to all this. You don't know what it means to me.

Marlow

It must be awfully hard.

Jim

It's hell. I couldn't clear out. The skipper did that. It's well enough in his case. I couldn't and I wouldn't. It wouldn't do for me. You see, my father really believed in me. He fancied me as a sailor. By now it's in the London papers and he's seen it. I can never face him again. I could never explain. He wouldn't understand.

Marlow

What will you do?

Jim

I don't know. I don't know where to turn. My license will be canceled, of course. I don't know anything else but sailoring and I've no money. Maybe I could become a quartermaster?

Marlow

Do you think you would?

(Jim gets up and walks to the veranda railing.)

Jim

Why the hell did you have to say that? You've been very understanding up to now. If I hadn't made that mistake, you know. (laughs)

Marlow

That mistake is no laughing matter to me.

Jim

That doesn't mean for one minute that I admit the cap fits.

Marlow

No?

Jim

No! (pause) Do you know what you would have done? Do you? And you don't think yourself a cur? (pause) Don't you see it's all in being ready? I wasn't. Not then. I don't mean to rationalize it or excuse myself. I'd just like someone to understand. You. Why not you?

Marlow

I'm trying.

Jim (bursting out)

My God, what a chance I missed.

Marlow

If you has stuck to the ship, you mean. Yes, it's too bad you didn't know beforehand.

Jim

God damn it! I tell you there was nothing I could do. I was not afraid of death. Do you believe that?

Marlow

Yes. I do. But the emergency did frighten you. After all it's always the unexpected that happens.

Jim

Damn! And you know that goddam German called me a coward; it really makes me laugh.

(Jim laughs loudly.)

Marlow

You mustn't laugh that way with all these people about.

Jim

Oh, they'll think I'm drunk. What would you have done? You're so sure of yourself, now aren't you? What would you do if this veranda started to move. Just move a little under you. You'd leap into the jungle. You know you would. In one leap into those bushes.

Marlow (looking)

Well, I think I'd fall short by several feet, as far as that goes. How did that fellow die, Jim? The engineer?

Jim

I don't know for sure. He'd been sickly. He may have had a weak heart. (laughs) It's easy to see he didn't want to die, either. Droll, isn't it? I'll be damned if he wasn't fooled into killing himself. Fooled. No more, no less. Just as I.... Oh, if I had only stayed put with my hands in my pocket.

Marlow

A chance missed, eh?

Jim

Why don't you laugh? It was a joke hatched in hell. A weak heart! Sometimes I wish mine had been.

Marlow

Do you? I don't know what more you could wish for. (he pushes the whisky to Jim) Won't you have some more?

Jim

Don't you think I can tell you what there is to tell without liquor?

Marlow

I was only being polite. Well, go on.

Jim

When I landed in that boat they couldn't forgive me for it. They hated me. They thought I was George. They were surprised all right.

(The captain and the two other men stand at a distance.)

Engineer (to Jim)

What the hell are you doing here? A gentleman? Too much of a gentleman to lend a hand. Too dignified to participate in saving his life. You finally came out of your trance, did you, you goddamn sneak? You aren't fit to live.

Captain

Vell, vell, *schwein*. So you finally had the courage to jump? You are not wanted here. Ve kindly request that you leave our ship the way you came.

Engineer

What's to prevent us from tossing you overboard, you bastard?

Jim

Just try.

Captain

Too good for you.

Jim

I only wish they had tried.

Marlow

What an extraordinary affair.

Jim

Not bad, eh?

Captain

What did you do to George? Did you kill him? You rotten sneak. Where is he?

Jim

How the hell should I know?

Captain

You murdering coward.

Jim

Shut up. The others You killed him. You killed him.

Captain

No, but I'll kill you all if you don't shut up.

(Jim jumps up and they retreat.)

Engineer

You aren't going to hit a man with a broken arm, are you? You're no gentleman.

(The captain lunges forward.)

Jim

Come on.

(The captain retreats. Then the captain and the engineer fade into the night. Jim stands there waving his fists.)

Marlow

Steady. Steady.

Jim

What? Uh. I'm not excited. (realizing) Sorry. Clumsy

of me. I dare say I'm not as steady now as I was then. I was ready for anything.

Marlow

You had a lively time of it in that boat.

Jim

I was ready then. After the ship's lights disappeared anything might have happened in that boat and the world no wiser. I felt it and I was pleased. The feeling thrilled me. There was no law, no fear to restrain me.

Marlow

Well, what happened?

Jim

Absolutely nothing. I meant business and they meant noise. Nothing happened. I wouldn't let them near me for a while because I didn't trust them. They started saying they didn't mean me any harm. I leave it to you! No harm. What more could they have done to me? You do see it, don't you? They were too much for me. Say something, will you?

Marlow

You've been sorely tried.

Jim

More than is fair. And then they wanted to get chummy. Make the best of it. They didn't mean a damn thing. They misunderstood about George. I was at the tiller you see, and they'd lost the rudder. It was comic. They kept looking at the tiller and then at me. They were very sorry. And pretty soon they were trying to think up a tale to tell about what happened. I wasn't having any part of it. And yet, we were all in the same boat.

(Jim paces up and down with his hands in his pockets.)

The captain said I'd die of the sun if I didn't watch out. I was thinking about it.

Marlow

You mean to say, you'd been deliberating whether you would die?

Jim

Yes. It had come to that. Don't you believe it?

Marlow

Yes, I believe it. I believe almost anything you tell me.

Jim

You don't know what it means to me to be believed, to

be able to make a clean breast of it to an older man. It's so hard to understand. It wasn't like a fight.

Marlow

That's for sure.

Jim

I was just uncertain what to do. If I had known. If there'd been one thing, I could have done it. But there wasn't.

Marlow

Ah, yes. You were uncertain.

Jim

Well, there wasn't. There's a very fine line between the right and wrong of this thing.

Marlow

That's true enough. How much more did you want?

Jim

Suppose I hadn't? I mean suppose I had stuck to the ship longer? How much longer? Say a minute. If I hadn't jumped for the boat? If I had waited a little longer until it seemed absolutely certain she was going down and then jumped. That would have been all right. And then I could have tried to save my life, and then it would have been all right, wouldn't it?

Marlow

Yes, you could have saved yourself then. You'd have been saved.

Jim

Yes. But the truth is, I really wasn't thinking about saving myself when I jumped. I just did it. Don't you believe me? You got me here to talk. You said you would believe me.

Marlow

Of course, I do.

Jim

Forgive me. I would not have been able to say these things to you if you were not a gentleman. And I am one, too. You still don't understand why I didn't run away afterwards. Well, it's simple. I wasn't going to be frightened of what I had done. Ashamed, yes. Not frightened. My heart is not weak. (he thumps his chest)

Marlow

No.

Jim

If I had stuck to the ship, I would have done my best to be saved. The line is so fine...between what I did and what I should have done.

Marlow

It's difficult to see a hair at midnight.

Jim

If I had...had wanted to run out on the ship, I could have. I could have gone with the others, helped them, so forth. No one would have known. That made it no easier. I didn't want all this talk. No one could have made me talk. I'm not afraid to tell. I wasn't afraid to think, either. I looked it in the face. I wasn't going to run away. At first I might have. But I wasn't going to be like them. I had to live the truth down, alone and by myself. A lie wouldn't help.

Marlow

What did it prove after all?

Jim

I was sick of life. But running was no way out. I believe it would have ended in nothing. What do you believe?

Marlow

What will you do?

Jim

Wait for another chance.

Marlow

Another chance?

Jim

The boat picked us up before sunset. They lied. I said nothing. Only I knew.

Marlow

You said nothing.

Jim

What was there to say? I was in the same boat with them. That's what I had to live down. It was like cheating the dead.

Marlow

And there were no dead.

Jim

That doesn't matter.

Marlow

Perhaps not.

Jim

Dead or not, I couldn't get clear. I had to live, didn't I?

Marlow

Yes, if you take it that way.

Jim

The inquiry was a relief. I knew I had to face it out. I couldn't hide and say nothing. And maybe forget it had ever happened. If only there had been a light on that ship. If there had, I would have swum back. Do you doubt it?

Marlow

No. Perhaps, if I gave you some money, you could make your way somewhere else.

Jim

Alone, I could. But not until after the inquiry is over.

Marlow

My offer is unconditional. I neither demand nor expect any sort of gratitude. You can repay me whenever convenient.

Jim

Very good of you. But I can't.

Marlow

I don't see what good there is in your staying here. Why lick the dregs?

Jim

I'm damned if I know why I must. I've tried to tell you. But, after all, it's my trouble. I jumped, but I don't know why.

Marlow

Better men than you have found it expedient to jump at times.

Jim

I'm not good enough to run. I've got to face it out. And I'm fighting it now.

(There is silence for a while.)

Jim

I had no idea it was so late. You must have had enough of this and so have I.

Marlow

What will you do afterwards?

Jim

Go to the dogs as likely as not.

Marlow

Remember, I'd like very much to see you again before you go.

Jim

Why not? This damned thing won't make me invisible. No such luck.

(Jim goes away. The guests return.)

Marlow

I could hear the gravel crunching under his feet. He was running, absolutely running. Nowhere to go and he was not yet four and twenty. He had confessed himself to me as if I could give absolution. Although what good it would have done him, I can't see. This was a case which no solemn deception could palliate. His maker had left him to his own devices, stunned by the discovery he had made. The discovery about himself. And he was trying to explain it to the only man capable of appreciating it in all its tremendous magnitude, himself. He didn't try to minimize its importance; therein lies his destruction. He stood before me, hoping that age and wisdom could find a remedy against the pain of truth. Oh, he was an imaginative beggar. He had no time to regret what he had lost, he was so concerned over what he had failed to obtain. It was tragic. And who was I to refuse him pity?

Guest

You are so subtle, Marlow.

Marlow

And all he needed was a fair chance. It was enormous. Enormous. Since he had been so high he had been preparing himself for all possible emergencies. He was ready to die. That is not very rare. But it is rare to see a man willing to fight a losing battle to the very end. In me he wanted an accomplice. I was being persuaded into understanding the unconceivable. A very discomforting sensation. I began to see the convention, the lie that lurks in all truth and the essential sincerity of falsehood. It was strange, for despite it all, he was one of us.

Guest

He took it to heart, then?

Marlow

Very much.

Guest

Then, he is no good. A man must see things exactly as they are or give in at once. I made it a practice never to take anything to heart.

Marlow

Yes, you see things as they are.

Guest

What happened at the inquiry?

Marlow

There were several questions before the court. The court found the *Patna* was unseaworthy. Yet it was declared that the ship was navigated with good and seaman-like care. It was unable to arrive at a cause for the accident. A derelict was suspected.

Guest

Did he keep his license?

Marlow

All licenses were canceled.

Guest

What became of him?

Marlow

I got him a job with some friends of mine as a ship's chandler in Bombay. That lasted for about six months. An unfortunate incident occurred which made him leave his job.

Jim (shouting)

I couldn't stand his confounded impudence. I couldn't stand the familiarity of the little beast. I had to leave!

Marlow (to Jim)

Just because that little engineer showed up in the same port, what did it matter? He didn't bother you, did he?

Jim

Oh, no. He didn't tell his story or mine. He didn't

accuse me. But I couldn't stand being anywhere near him. So I gave your name for a reference and now I'm with Egstrom A. Blake, Chandlers, in Calcutta.

Marlow (to guests)

And a few months later, we met. (to Jim) What have you got to say for yourself?

Jim

What I wrote you in my letter, nothing more.

Marlow

Did the fellow blab?

Jim

Oh, no. He made it confidential between us. He was damnably mysterious whenever he came around. He'd wink at me. Wink at me! And he called me a gentleman. I had to leave.

Marlow (to guests)

And very soon his past caught up with him again and he moved on a little bit further south. And a little bit further east. That was the pattern that developed. It went on this way for about two years. I decided I must do something to help him.

Guest

What did you do?

Marlow

I contacted an old friend named Stein. He ran a trading company with posts in the interior of Borneo. This was Jim's great opportunity to get away from his past forever. The time was to come when I should see him loved, trusted, admired, with a legend of strength surrounding his name like a Greek hero. He went native. He was to taste the joy of it, but in the end to die of it. I don't mean to say that I regret my action, yet the idea forces itself upon me that if he had not made so much of his disgrace, it would have been his guilt alone that mattered. A slightly coarser nature would not have noticed the disgrace. A coarser one still would not have even felt the guilt.

Guest

So you contacted that man Stein?

(Marlow gets up. To the right of the stage, a small office and a desk at which sits an old man.)

Stein

So you see me. So, only one specimen like this they have in your London and then no more. (holds up a butterfly) To my small native town this collection I shall bequeath. Something of me. The best.

Marlow

Marvelous. Marvelous. A masterpiece.

Stein

Look, the beauty. But that is nothing. Observe the accuracy, the harmony. And so fragile, and so strong, and so exact. That is nature. The balance of colossal forces. This wonder, this masterpiece of nature, the great artist.

Marlow

I never heard an entomologist go on like this before. If this is a masterpiece, what of man?

Stein

Man amazes, but he is not a masterpiece. Perhaps the artist was a little mad, hmm, what do you think? Sometimes it seems to me that man has come where he is not wanted. Where there is no place for him. For if not, why should he desire everything, run about talking about the stars, and disturbing the grass?

Marlow

And catching butterflies.

Stein

Exactly. Sit down. I captured this specimen myself one fine morning. You can't bemoan the feeling. It was a long time ago, back in Patusan. There was a great enemy of mine in those days. It was like feudal times. He was a great noble and a greater rascal, roaming about with a band of thugs. I left my home, cantering around for four or five miles. There had been rain in the night. But the mists had gone up and the face of the earth was clean. Suddenly somebody fired a volley of shots at me. I hear the bullets sing in my ear and my hat jumps off my head. This wanted a little management. I pretended to fall forward on my horse, dead. I clutched the horse's mane. Quietly, I drew my revolver. After all, there were only seven of these rascals. I slid down from my horse. Soon they got up from the grass and started running with their sarongs tucked up, waving spears and rifles, and yelling to each other to catch the horse because I was dead. I let them come as close as that door and then: Bang, bang, bang. I got three, the others ran and I sat alone and looked at these three corpses. I observed a shadow pass over the forehead of one of them. It was the shadow of this. (gestures to the butterfly) Look at the form of the wing. This species flies high. I lost him in the sun. I rise, revolver in hand. Shading my eyes with the other hand, I approach. Carefully. Very, very carefully. At last I find him alighting on a small heap of dirt. At once my heart began to beat quick. This species flies high with a strong flight. I saw him fluttering away; I think, is it possible? And then I lose him. Holding my revolver and carrying my hat in my other hand, I looked for him all over. At last I saw him about ten feet away. At once my heart began to pound. One step, steady. Another step, plop, I got him with my hat. I was shaking like a leaf: not from fear, but from joy at having caught him. The perfect specimen. I had to sit down. Yes, my good friend, on that day I wanted for nothing. Phoe. (blowing out a match) The work is making great progress. I have this rare specimen (gestures) and what is your good news?

Marlow

To tell the truth, I came here to describe a specimen.

Stein

A butterfly?

Marlow

Nothing so perfect. A man, of a sort.

Stein

Ah, so. Well, I am a man, too.

Marlow

I have a friend. He was the chief mate on the *Patna*.

Stein

Ah, the *Patna*. I have heard of that affair. Very interesting.

Marlow

He was not like the rest. He was one of us.

Stein

Ah, so.

Marlow

He believes himself capable of doing great things if he could only make a fresh start.

Stein

A clean slate, did he say? As if each word of our destinies were not graven in imperishable characters. He is romantic, I understand very well.

Marlow

What is the remedy?

Stein

There is only one. One thing alone can save us from ourselves.

Marlow

Yes, the question is not the cure, but how to live.

Stein

How to be? Ah, how to be? We want in so many ways to be. This magnificent butterfly finds a little heap of dirt and sits still on it, but man on his little heap of mud will never be still on it. He wants to be. And he wants to be so. He wants to be a saint and he wants to be a devil. And every time he shuts his eyes he sees himself as a very fine fellow...as fine as he can never be: in a dream. And because you can't always keep your eyes shut there comes the real trouble. I tell you, my friend, it is not good to find you cannot make your dream come true for the reasons you are not strong enough or clever enough; *ja*, all the time you are such a fine fellow, too? How can that be, hah? A man that is falls into a dream like a man falling into the sea. And he drown. No, I tell you the way is to the destructive element submit yourself. That is how to be. I follow the dream. Tonight, you sleep. And in the morning we shall do something practical. Practical. He is a romantic. So romantic and that is very bad, but very good, too.

Marlow

But, is he?

Stein

Surely, by inward pain he knows himself. And that is what makes him exist for you and me.

Marlow

Perhaps he is, but I am sure you are.

Stein

Well, I exist, too.

Marlow

Yes, and amongst other things you dreamed of a butterfly. But, when one morning your dream came your way, you did not let the splendid opportunity escape.

Stein

No, not that one. But, do you know how many others?

Marlow

But he did not catch this one.

Stein

Everyone has one or two like that. And that is the trouble. The great trouble. So, sleep well, my friend, and tomorrow we must do something practical. Practical.

Marlow

What do you have in mind?

Stein

I don't suppose you have ever heard of a place called Patusan? It doesn't matter.

Marlow

That's where you came from, isn't it?

Stein

Yes, I dare say, I know more about Patusan than anyone else. Even the government. It's a jungle, physical and moral. He won't mind a jungle, so much the better for him. He wants a hole to hide in, no better place. This man who runs my trading post there is a scoundrel. His name is Cornelius. I only kept him there because of his wife who was very dear to me. I kept him on because of her daughter, when she died. It was her girl, not his. He insisted she call him father. It was "a revenge" shall we say. But I can't keep him any longer.

Marlow

You think Jim would be suited for this?

Stein

That remains to be seen. I will give him a ring to my friend Doramin who is a prince out there. He is my friend. He saved my life and I saved his. He will do anything for me. The ring is a sort of letter of introduction. I will also give him a letter to Cornelius. This is all I will give him.

Marlow

Then, let me give him an old revolver of mine.

Stein

And now that we have done something practical tonight...let us go to bed.

(Marlow walks back to the veranda and sits back among the guests.)

First Guest

Well, then, what happened then?

Marlow

For several years I did not see him, but I heard of him.

Second Guest

As he said you would.

Marlow

Yes. Indeed, after he arrived he soon became a legend. He became the supreme ruler there. He was looked on as a god. He overcame unbelievable odds, stripped the rajah of his power, and they loved him for it. They loved him for it.

Second Guest

Did you ever see him again?

Marlow

Yes. Several years later. I had received letters from him, but they told little. I arrived on a hot tropical night after sailing inland on a little schooner. These schooners came after Jim's arrival and because of him. Before that it was worth your life to venture inland.

(Marlow gets up and walks back toward the right of the stage.)

CURTAIN

ACT II

Stein's house has disappeared and has been replaced with a native hut, palm trees and a lush jungle background.

Marlow

Greetings, Jim. This is glorious.

Jim

Yes.

Marlow

You have had your opportunity!

Jim

Have I? Well, yes, I suppose so. I have got back my confidence in myself. A good name. Yet, sometimes I wish...no. I'll hold what I've got. I can't expect anything more. Not out here. This is my limit because nothing less will do. Look at those houses. There's not one where I am not trusted. I told you I would hang on.

Ask anyone. I am all right now.

Marlow

I was sure you would be.

Jim

Were you?

Marlow

Tell me all about it. I want to hear it from your own lips.

Jim

It's really quite simple. I paddled my way upstream till I got, oh, down there a ways. Then I found myself surrounded by buggers. I called them buggers then. Today, I call them my people. Frankly, I was scared. It's a good thing I forgot to load your gun.

Marlow

Why?

Jim

Because I would have shot somebody and then it would have been all over. So, I just stood still because I had to and told them to take me to the rajah. Everyone admired my iron nerves. They were shocked and did what I said.

Marlow

It was as simple as that?

Jim

Oh, no. They put me in that stockade over there. I was held prisoner for three days.

Marlow

What then?

Jim

I decided I didn't like it up there too much and to make it to the opposite bank. Which I did. I almost got killed, but I made it across. Then I presented myself to Doramin with my ring.

Marlow

And?

Jim

And Doramin, with his son Dain Waris who is my dearest friend, helped me to organize some resistance. So you know, in addition to the rajah, there was a band of pirate Arabs holed up on that peak over there. Doramin is chief of the immigrants from the Celebes. They're civilized to an extent and reasonably friendly, about sixty families with dependents. They muster about two hundred men. He's their chief. Elected, you understand. The men are intelligent, a bit revengeful, yet very courageous and loyal. Make a friend of them and they're yours for life. They were opposed to the rajah. In a flash I understood that they had to act unless they wanted to sink, one after another, between the rajah and the Arab vagabonds. So, without the weight of Doramin's authority and his son's fiery enthusiasm, I couldn't have succeeded. Dain Waris was the first to believe in me. He persuaded his father. We organized a party of fifty men and stormed the heights. Right up the cliff. They never knew what hit them. We didn't lose a man. And scattered the Arabs, killing maybe a dozen.

Marlow

You must have enjoyed it.

Jim

It was tremendous, spectacular, immense. Simply immense. You can't imagine. Think what it is to me. And can you think I want to leave? It would be harder than dying. Don't laugh. I feel every day that I am trusted. That no one can—not for a minute—no one has a right—you understand, of course.

Marlow

Stein intends that you should take over the post in your own right. On any conditions that would make the transaction agreeable to you.

Jim

I really don't want to do that.

Marlow

You've earned it. Stein isn't making you a gift.

Jim

No, but, I'd rather just be his helper. I feel prouder of that. Prouder than I would working for myself for some reason.

Marlow

But you really have to give in on this point, Jim.

Jim

I'll think about it; I'll write to Stein.

Marlow

Well, that's the best I can do for the present, I suppose.

(At this point natives start pouring in from all sides. Presently the rajah appears amidst his court.)

Jim

Ah, the rajah has turned up for our monthly ceremony.

Marlow

Ceremony?

Jim

I drink tea with the rajah.

(A native passes tea from a samovar to the rajah and Jim. There are mutual bows and exchanges of ceremonial affection. A cup is also offered to Marlow.)

Jim

You needn't, really.

Marlow

You mean that…why do you expose yourself to such stupid risks? (drinks)

Jim

It's the barest chance, you know. The barest chance. I really don't think he would try to poison me.

(The rajah smiles and bows uncomprehendingly.)

Jim

I think he's altogether too scared for that.

Marlow

He's scared enough. Anyone can see that.

Jim

If I am to do any good here, and preserve my position, then I must take the risk. I take tea with the rajah once a month at least, and sometimes more often if the situation is troublesome. Many people trust me to do that for them. You see, he is afraid of me, that's just it. Most likely he is afraid of me because I am not afraid of his tea. Or perhaps, I should say that while I am quite afraid of his tea, I drink it anyway and don't show it.

(The ceremony ends abruptly. Almost as abruptly as it began. The rajah and the natives withdraw.)

Jim

I always do it in public. It's no good if I do it in private. It's a ritual of my power here.

Marlow

It's a bitter price to pay.

Jim

Oh, the tea is quite good, really. Let's forget that. Come, you must meet Doramin and his wife. And Dain Waris. Then you shall meet Jewel. Speak of the devil, here is Doramin now.

(Doramin is a massive old man, huge, corpulent, but dignified.)

Doramin

Ah, you are the friend of Tuan Jim. You must be my guest.

Marlow

It shall be my pleasure.

Jim

I must leave you anyway. You shall get acquainted.

(Jim goes.)

Doramin

It is good that there is such a man as Jim in these parts, in these times. In the old days, I could use my strength, but now I have grown old and tired. In Jim, I have unbounded confidence.

Marlow

I understand your son thinks very highly of Jim.

Doramin

Indeed he does. I have only one wish. And that is that Tuan Jim would promise. One word would be enough.

Marlow

Promise what?

Doramin

Well. It is a subject difficult to speak of. I am anxious for the future of my country and for the future of my son. The land remains where God has put it, but white men come to us and go in a little while. They go away. Those they leave behind do not know when to look for their return. They go to their own land, their own people. And so, this white man, too, will go away. I want him to designate Dain Waris, my son, as the leader who will take his place. If he does not do so before he goes, it may be difficult for Dain Waris to assert himself in the future.

Marlow

You need not worry. Jim will never leave.

Doramin (strangely)

This is very good news, indeed, that you give to me. Why will he never leave? Why has a man so young wandered so far from his home, never to return, and gone through so many dangers? Not for the sake of adventure alone. Has he no kinfolk there?

Marlow

He has a father.

Doramin

No other kinsmen?

Marlow

Brothers and sisters.

Doramin

Has he no position in his own country?

Marlow

No. That he has not. No, he will never, never leave.

(Jim returns. Doramin scrutinizes Jim as if seeing him for the first time.)

Jim

Ah, I have finally found Jewel. She is waiting for you at the hut. You must come and meet her.

Doramin

And then, you must come to see me, for I will be proud to entertain you. I have many questions to ask you. Many questions. (exits)

Jim

Come and meet Jewel. You know, you probably won't understand this—it's not what you're thinking.

Marlow

Have I said anything!

Jim

You're polite. But, you see, I'm...we're serious. I can't tell you what I owe her. You see, I don't want you to think...to misunderstand from appearances.

Marlow

I wasn't thinking anything. And, as for appearances—

Jim

Yes, yes, I know you're a very sophisticated man and all that, but really, you can't understand quite what she means to me. That fellow Cornelius who makes her call him father...he used to make her cry. And he mismanaged the post, too. He's a sneak. He embezzled quite a bit from Stein. I found out about it, of course. But there was no point in reporting him. But he's been slinking around the house ever since. He tries to make her call him father. When she wouldn't, he called her mother a whore. Apparently she and Stein were lovers and Jewel is his daughter. And Jewel wouldn't let me shut his mouth for him. Then one night about a month after I became master here, he woke me up in the middle of the night and told me there were men outside who wanted to kill me. If I would give him $80 he'd get me out safe, "only eighty dollars." I told him to get out before I killed him. Then I went back to sleep. Then Jewel woke me up. She led me out of the house and told me there were men in the stockade waiting to kill me. She brought a torch with her. They were inside the hut. She wanted me to run away, but I wouldn't do it. I told her to go to Doramin, but she wouldn't do that. I don't want to make it sound particularly heroic, but I think they were more frightened of me than I was of them. Jewel wouldn't go. When they heard me coming, they hid under some mats inside the storage house. I told her to thrust her torch in the window, then I went in with my pistol. I saw two right away and killed them and the other two surrendered. You see now why I feel the way

I do towards her. She had watched all night, you know. She was very much in love with me. She's necessary to my existence now. It's wonderful, but frightening, too.

Marlow

Don't hurt her.

Jim

I won't. I shall never leave. I have not forgotten why I came here. Ask them here, who is just, who is true, who is to be trusted with their lives, they will say Tuan Jim. And yet, they can never know the real truth. (brightening) Come, I haven't done so badly?

Marlow

Not so badly at all.

Jim

But all the same, you wouldn't like to have me aboard your own ship.

Marlow

Damn you, stop it.

Jim

You see. Only try to tell that to them. They'd call you

a liar. And so I can stand my knowledge of myself and your feelings for me because of how they feel.

Marlow

For them you shall always remain an unsolvable mystery.

Jim

Mystery? Well then, let it be so. But a mystery that remains among them. Besides, aren't all men mysteries?

(The scene darkens and Jim exits. Then Marlow enters alone, walks by the hut. As he does so, he is stopped by Jewel, who puts her hand on his arm and restrains him.)

Jewel

Do not take him away from me.

(Jewel's speech is stilted. Correct, but strongly accented.)

Marlow

I haven't come for that.

Jewel

Why did you come then?

Marlow

Friendship. To see him again. Business, too. I rather want him to stay.

Jewel

They always leave us.

Marlow

Nothing will separate Jim from Patusan.

Jewel

He swore to me.

Marlow

Did you ask him to?

Jewel

Never! No, never. That night, that night. After I flung the torch in the water because he was looking at me and the danger was over. He promised me he would never abandon me. I asked him to leave me. He said that he could not. That it was impossible. He trembled as he spoke. I felt him tremble. I told him to leave me. I fell at his feet. He raised me up. He lifted me up. And I could struggle no more. I did not want to die weeping, therefore I wanted him to go.

Marlow

You did not want to die weeping?

Jewel

Like my mother. My mother wept bitterly before she died, for Mr. Stein was not here. I was alone with her but Cornelius was outside screaming to be let in. She screamed that he should not be let in. The tears fell from her eyes and then she died.

(Suddenly Cornelius emerges from the shadows.)

Cornelius

Your mother was a devil. A deceitful devil, and you, too, are a devil.

Jewel

Go away.

Cornelius

I am a respectable man. And what are you? Tell me. What are you? What are you? You think I am going to bring up somebody's bastard and not be treated with respect? You should be thankful that I let you stay. Come say, "Yes, father." No. You wait a while. I'll fix you yet.

Marlow

You get out of here and get out of here now.

Cornelius

Honorable sir, honorable sir, how was I to know? Who is he, what could he do to make the people believe him? What did Mr. Stein mean, sending me a boy like that to talk big to the natives and to talk like that to me? Me, a trusted retainer. I was ready to save him for only eighty dollars. Only eighty dollars. Why didn't the fool go? Was I to run the risk of getting myself stabbed for the sake of a stranger without being compensated. He groveled in the spirit before me with his body. What's eighty dollars? An insignificant sum to give a defenseless old man ruined for life by a dead bitch.

Marlow (making a threatening gesture)

I'll tell Jim about this, even if she won't. Now, get out of here.

(The girl tries to restrain him.)

Marlow

Don't let him bother you.

Jewel

He is of no consequence now. It is Jim with whom I

am concerned. And you must answer me. He swore he would never leave me. He swore to me.

Marlow

And is it possible that you, you do not believe him?

Jewel

Other men have sworn the same thing to other women. My father did.

Marlow

Your father, too. Ah, but Jim is different, he is not like that.

Jewel

Why is Jim different, is he better?

Marlow

Yes. On my word, he is.

Jewel

Is he more true?

Marlow

Yes.

Jewel

More true than any other man?

Marlow

Nobody here would dream of doubting his word. Nobody would dare. Except you.

Jewel

Is he more brave?

Marlow

Fear will never drive him away from you. Look, what has he been telling you? He has told you something, hasn't he? What is it he told you?

Jewel

Do you think I can tell you? How am I to know? There is something he says he can never forget.

Marlow

So much the better for you.

Jewel

What is it? He says he has been afraid. How can I believe this? Am I a mad insane woman to believe this? You all remember something. You all go back to it. What is it? Will you tell me? What is this thing? Is it alive? Is it dead? I hate it. It is cruel. Has it a face and voice, this calamity?

Marlow

Calm yourself.

Jewel

Will he see it? Will he hear it? In his sleep, perhaps he cannot see me. And then get up and walk out. I shall never forgive him. My mother forgave, but I never will. Will it be a sign? A call? Will it be another woman?

Marlow

There is no other woman for Jim but you, Jewel. You have nothing to fear on that score. I don't believe a sign, a fear, a call, anything can tear him from you. Nothing living or dead could tear him from your side. Besides who would want to?

Jewel

That is what he told me.

Marlow

He told you the truth.

Jewel

Nothing? Then, why did you come to us from out there? He speaks of you too often. You frighten me. Do you...do you want him?

Marlow

I shall never come again. And I don't want him. No one wants him.

Jewel

No one?

Marlow

No one. You believe him to be strong, wise, courageous, great. Why don't you trust him, too? I will go away soon and that's the last you'll ever see of me. No one from the outside will trouble you again. The outside world, that you don't know, is too big to miss him. Don't you understand? Too big. You've got his heart. You must feel that. You must know that.

Jewel

Yes, I know he loves me. I know that.

Marlow

The outside world does not want him. Why don't you

believe it?

Jewel

Why doesn't it want him? Why? Tell me! Why? Speak!

Marlow

You really want to know?

Jewel

Yes.

Marlow

Because he is not good enough.

Jewel

That is the very thing he said. You lie. You both lie.

Marlow

Hear me out. Nobody, nobody is good enough.

Jewel

I don't believe you. I don't trust you. I don't trust him.

(Jewel hurries away. Jim enters and spies her retreating figure.)

Jim

What, no lights? What are you doing in the dark, you two? Hello, girl.

Jewel

Hello, boy.

(Jewel and Jim go off together. Marlow retreats.)

Jim

We'll see you later, Marlow.

(Cornelius stealthily reenters.)

Cornelius

Honorable sir. Honorable sir.

Marlow (furious)

What do you want? Why don't you just crawl back into the swamp?

Cornelius

I would have saved him, honorable sir. I would have saved him for only eighty dollars.

Marlow

He saved himself without your help. He forgave you, so why don't your forgive him.

(Cornelius starts to laugh.)

Marlow (irritated)

What are you laughing at?

Cornelius

Don't be deceived, honorable sir. He has saved himself. That's good. He knows nothing. Nothing whatever. He is a fool. A big fool. What does he know, honorable sir? He is no more than a little child. Like a little child. A little child. Ah, honorable sir, I mean nothing. My great misfortunes have overwhelmed me. Pay no attention to what I say. I don't mean anything by it. Sir, you do not know what it is to be ruined, broken down, trampled upon by a little slut.

Marlow

Shut your mouth.

Cornelius

If only he would make me an honorable, moderate provision, honorable sir. A suitable compensation for all that he has taken away from me. If you would only intercede on my behalf, honorable sir. Every gentleman made a provision when the time came to go home.

Marlow

In this case, Mr. Cornelius, the time shall never come.

Cornelius

What?

Marlow

Why, haven't you heard him say so yourself? He will never go home.

Cornelius

Oh, this is too much. Never go. He? He who comes here, devil knows from where, devil knows why, to trample on me till I die. Trample like this. Patience. Patience. (laughs) We shall see. We shall see. He comes here to steal from me. Everything, everything, everything. Just like her mother. Exactly. And her face, too. In her face. The little bitch. And he wasn't afraid. Ah, he is a little child. A little child, a little child. (wanders off)

(The lights dim out completely. When they rise, Marlow is back with is companions on the verandah.)

Marlow

And so. I lost him.

First Guest

Did that little runty Cornelius do him in?

Marlow

No. But he figured in his downfall. I never saw Jim again. It all happened very suddenly, as in a Greek tragedy. In one rotation of the sun, he was at the peak of his power, and by nightfall he was a dead man, ruined and disgraced.

Guest

What happened? How did you come to know of it?

Marlow

I learned about it later from Stein. The girl, Jewel, was there, and Jim's servant Tam-iTam.

(At this point, Stein's study becomes visible on the right of the stage and Tam-iTam, Jewel and Stein stand like a Greek chorus. Marlow walks to them.)

Marlow

How did it happen?

Stein

You shall hear.

Tam-iTam

He would not fight.

Jewel

He was false.

Stein

No, no, no, my poor child. He was true, true, true. Not false. No. No. You do not understand.

Jewel

What have I done?

Marlow

You always mistrusted him.

Jewel

He was like the others.

Stein

Terrible. Terrible. What can one do for her?

Jewel

I hate him.

Marlow

You must forgive him.

Stein

We all want to be forgiven.

Jewel

He shall have no tears from me. Not one tear. Never, never. I will not. He left me as if I were worse than death. He fled as if driven by some accursed thing he had heard in his sleep. He could see my face. He was looking at me. He could hear my voice and hear my grief. And yet he went. When I used to sit at his feet with my cheek against his knee and his hand on my head the curse of cruelty and madness was already within him waiting for the day and then the day came. Before the sun had set he could not see me any more. He was made blind and deaf and without pity. As you all are, you men. He shall have no tears from me. (weeping)

Stein

Someday she will understand.

Marlow

Will you explain?

Cornelius (entering)

He was like a child. I told you that he was like a child, the fool.

Stein

It began when a man named Brown and a crew of cutthroats sailed up the river. They were starving and fleeing from a Spanish patrol boat. They were pirates. They had to have food. Jim was up country when they arrived in their little canoe. About a dozen men. They stormed the heights successfully.

Jewel

I told the people to attack. Dain Waris and I were ready to lead the attack but Doramin said we must wait for Jim. I wanted to attack them immediately. Oh, if only I had not listened.

Stein

Doramin feared for his son's life. So he waited for Jim.

Marlow

What happened when he arrived?

Stein

Before he got there Cornelius had made contact with Brown. That was Jim's undoing.

(The scene blacks out. When the lights go up we are on the heights. Brown, in command of his men, is standing on the ridge protected by a rock. There is shouting.)

Cornelius (voice)

Let a man come see you, please. A poor ruined old man. A white man.

Brown

Come on, then. But come alone, mind. Come on, you're safe.

(Cornelius scurries up and bows to Brown.)

Cornelius

The rajah humbly requests that you explain why you are here, honorable sir.

Brown

Well, you can tell him we've come for food—and anything else around here worth carrying off. And by God, we'll do it or die trying. Now you go tell this to this rajah.

Cornelius

It is not the rajah who will make trouble for you, it is Lord Jim.

Brown

Jim? Who is this Jim? That's not enough for a man's name.

Cornelius

That's what they call him.

Brown

And who is he? What is he? Where does he come from? Is he an Englishman?

Cornelius

Yes, yes, he's English, as I am. He is a fool, all you have to do is kill him and then you are king here. Everything belongs to him. The rajah will cooperate with you, I believe. But you must act before he returns. Once he gets here, you're dead in the water.

Brown

I don't see why he can't be made to share with somebody here, before too long.

Cornelius

No. No. The proper way is to kill him the first chance you get. Then you can do what you like. I am an old man and have lived many years. I give you a friend's advice. The rajah does not like Jim. He is afraid of Jim, but as long as Jim is alive he will not aid you. If you kill Jim, then he will aid you. He will bow down to you like he did to Jim. He is a coward, that rajah.

(More gunfire. At least one of the defenders is killed. Another is wounded and lies shrieking. Brown returns the fire, as do his men.)

Brown

Well, we got at least two of the buggers in return, but it is not a fair match. They must be at least two hundred to one. Two hundred to one. Listen, boys, strike terror. Terror, I tell you. Put the fear of God in them. That will show them what we can do.

(There is more shooting. Suddenly the shooting on the other side stops. Then Brown's men stop. A sudden silence.)

A Yankee

It's unnotcheral.

Jim (voice)

Let no one fire. Do you hear, on the hill? Do you understand English? Do you hear? Do you hear?

Cornelius

It's Lord Jim.

(Cornelius cowers with fear.)

Brown

I hear. Hold your fire, men. (to Cornelius) What does it mean? (to Jim) Speak. We understand.

(The natives beat their drums.)

Brown

What's all that about?

Cornelius

They're rejoicing at his return. He is a very great man. But all the same, he knows no more than a child. And so, they make a great noise to please him and would you—

Brown

Look here. How is one to get at him?

Cornelius

What do you mean? Simplest thing in the world. He'll come strolling over here to talk to you. Just like a fool. All you have to do is kill him. You'll see. You'll see. He's not afraid. Not afraid of anything. He will come and order you to leave his people alone. Everybody must leave his people alone. He is like a little child. He will make straight for you. Just kill him and you will frighten everybody so much that you can do whatever you like. Tell that tall man there to kill Jim.

Brown

Oh, shut the hell up.

(Jim comes, waving a white flag.)

Jim

Who are you?

Brown

My name is Brown. Captain Brown. Gentleman Brown. Who are you?

Jim

What made you come here?

Brown

Oh, you want to know? Well, it's no secret. Hunger. And what made you?

Jim (blushing)

That's my affair.

Brown

My man has you covered. You can see that.

Jim

I see it. But you can never escape here if you kill me.

Brown

Let us agree that we are both dead men and negotiate on that basis. I may be like a rat in a trap and so are my men, but we've been driven to it and even a rat can give a bite.

Jim

Not if you don't go near the trap till the rat is dead.

Brown

I thought you were a white man. Goddam it, you're not going to sip tea and count how many of us are dead, are you? Come on, bring your crowd along and we'll give you an open battle. Or else, let us go. You were a white man—once anyway—for all your talk of this being your people, and your being one with them. What the hell do you think you are? And who the devil do you think cares about you? What is it you've found here that's so goddam precious you don't want us to come down here and ruin your little racket? Is that it? You're two hundred to one and you don't have guts enough to fight! We'll give you something to remember before we're finished. You'll get us, yes, but we'll get a few of you. You talk about me, making a cowardly set upon your unoffending little people. What's that to me when I'm starving? But I'm no coward. So don't you be one. You bring them along or somehow we'll manage to send half your unoffending town to hell. We aren't going to go into the jungle and wander around for the ants to pick us off one by one. Oh, no.

Jim

You don't deserve a better fate. You've killed innocent men.

Brown

And what do you deserve? You that I find skulking here with your mouth full of pious responsibility, innocent lives, of your infernal duty. What do you know more of me than I know of you? How do I know where you came from? I came here for food, do you hear?

You may be worse than I for all I know. What did you ask for when you came? We don't ask you for anything but to give us a fair fight or let us go back where we came from.

Jim

I could fight you now. And I would let you shoot me now and welcome. This is as good a jumping off place for me as another, but it would be too easy. These are my men in the same boat and I am not the sort to jump out of trouble and leave them in the lurch.

Brown

Have we got to tell each other the story of our lives? Suppose you begin? No? Well, I am sure I don't want to hear. So keep it to yourself. I'm sure you're no better than I. A man doesn't go native for nothing. You talk like you should have wings so that you needn't touch the dirty earth. Well, it is dirty. And I haven't got wings. And neither have you. I'm here because I was afraid once in my life. Want to know what of? Of prison. A prison scares me. And I don't care if you know it, if it's any good to you. I'll be my own master till I die. I won't ask you what scared you into this hole, because I can see you aren't about to tell. Well, you've found pretty pickings. That's your luck and this is mine. The privilege to beg for the favor of being shot quickly or else to be allowed to go starve in my own way. Frankly, I'd just as soon fight. If you force us to fight, there's only one way we have a chance, considering the odds. We have to shoot anything living and fire everything right and left.

Jim

What about that man you killed?

Brown

Isn't that war? Besides, you got one of us. And you didn't have to listen to him dying for hours, screaming with pain all night. At any rate, it's a life for a life. Don't you understand, man, that when it comes to saving your life in the dark, you don't give a damn who else goes? One or a thousand.

Jim

Will you promise to leave the coast?

Brown

Of course, what else can I do?

Jim

And surrender your arms?

Brown

Surrender our arms? Are you crazy? Not until you

come and take them out of our hands. Do you think I'm insane? That and the rags I stand in are all I've got in the world. I expect to sell my life dear.

Jim

I don't know whether I have the power....

Brown

Get you? You don't know whether you have the power? And you want me to surrender my arms? That's rich! What do you mean, you don't have the power? Why did you come down here if you didn't have the power? To pass the time of day?

Jim

Very well. I'll give you either a clear road or a clear fight.

(Jim goes.)

Cornelius

Why didn't you kill him?

Brown

Because I told you, I could do better than that.

Cornelius

Never. I've lived here for years. I know.

Brown

You will see. I will get a clear road.

Cornelius

I could tell you something you would like to know. You did not kill him and what will you get for it? A clear road.

Brown

That's what I wanted.

Cornelius

You might have had money from the rajah, besides all the plunder, and now you get nothing.

Brown

You'd better clear out.

Cornelius

I could still tell you something you'd like to know.

Brown

Spill it. What's that?

Cornelius

I believe Dain Waris, Jim's friend, has led a party down river near your boat, on one of the islands.

Brown

So he intends to betray me?

Cornelius

Oh, no. If he promises you safety, they will not attack. They're just there to see you don't change your mind. He'll send a messenger to warn them not to attack you.

Brown

Well then?

Cornelius

There is a passage up behind one of these islands.

Brown

So he thinks I will be harmless, does he?

Cornelius

Yes, he is a fool, a little child. He came here and robbed me and made all the people believe in him. If something happened so that the people no longer believed in him, where would he be? The man who is down there on that little island is the very man who chased you up here when you first came. His name is Dain Waris. He's the son of the chieftain here. I could lead you so that you could sneak up on them. You must be quiet, for at one place you pass close to the camp. Very close.

Brown

Oh, we know how to be very quiet. Like little mice. Never fear.

(The scene shifts now to the council of war being held by Jim and his followers.)

Jim

It is my wish that these men go free. I can speak to you, Doramin, before all the others, for you know my heart as well as I know yours. Its greatest desire. And you know also that I have no thought but the people's good.

Doramin

But lives have been lost already.

Jim

Why lose more? You know, people, that your welfare is my welfare; your loss is my loss, your mourning is my mourning. We have fought side by side. You remember and I do not forget. You know this and you know my courage.

(The crowd murmurs approvingly.)

You know I have never deceived you in the many years we have dwelt together. I love the land and I love the people living in it with a very great love. I am ready to answer with my life for any harm that should befall you if the white men with the beards are allowed to go. These men are evil doers. But their destiny has been evil too. Have I ever advised you ill? Have my words ever brought suffering to you? It is best to let these men go. It would be a small gift to me, whom you have tried and found always true. I ask you to let them go.

Doramin

I say we should attack.

Jim

Then call in Dain Waris, your son, my friend, for in this I shall not lead.

Doramin

What is it but the taking of another hill?

Jewel

If you are afraid, let me lead.

Jim

No.

Jewel

Let me go. This is unseemly. Are they not cruel, blood-thirsty robbers bent on killing?

Jim

Let them be. Everyone shall be safe. Let them go because this is my best wisdom which has never deceived you.

Doramin

It is best then. Let them go.

Others

Let it be as Tuan Jim wishes. Let it be so.

(The crowd breaks up.)

Jim

Well, there's no rest for us, old girl, while our people are in danger. We are responsible for every life in the land.

Jewel

Yes, and that is why you should not let them go.

Jim

You're more a man than I am. If you and Dain Waris had your way, all those poor devils would be dead.

Jewel

They are very bad men.

Jim

Men act badly from time to time without being much worse than others.

(The scene changes. Jim is now talking across the river to Brown.)

Jim

You get the clear road. Start as soon as your boat floats on the morning tide. Let your men be careful, for on both sides of the river there will be well-armed men.

You should have no chance except that I don't believe you want bloodshed. (silence) You had better trust the current while the fog lasts. (silence) If you think it worth your while to wait a day down river, I'll try to send you some food. Bullock, or what ever I can.

Cornelius (to Brown)

Perhaps you shall get a small bullock. You'll get it if he said so. He always speaks the truth. He stole everything I had. I can see you're the kind of man to prefer a small bullock rather than the booty to be had here.

Brown

Shut up or I'll drown you in that damned little creek. I'll throw you in.

Cornelius

Then, how will you have your revenge?

Brown

Am I to believe you could really find that back way you spoke of?

Cornelius

Easily.

Brown

And you're not afraid to go with me?

Cornelius

It will be a pleasure, honorable sir.

(The scene changes. It is the stockade. Tam-iTam enters, panting.)

Tam-iTam

They have killed Dain Waris and many more.

Jewel

Shut the gates. What will we do about Doramin?

Tam-iTam

We have all the powder in Patusan. He cannot attack us.

Jewel

What is the matter?

Tam-iTam

It is I, Tam-iTam, with tidings that cannot wait. This, Tuan, is a day of evil, an accursed day.

Jim

What has happened?

Tam-iTam

Those evil men killed Dain Waris and all our party on the shore. They took us by surprise. Cornelius led them by a roundabout route.

Jim

What has become of him?

Tam-iTam

Twice I struck, Tuan. When he beheld me approaching, he cast himself violently upon the ground and made a great outcry, kicking, he screeched like a frightened hen when he felt the point, then he lay still and lay staring at me while his life went out of his eyes.

Jim

And the other white men?

Tam-iTam

They are gone, Tuan.

Jim

Give Tam-iTam something to eat.

Tam-iTam

Why do you stand here? Waste no time. Forgive me, Tuan, but, but....

Jim

What?

Tam-iTam

It is not safe for thy servant to go out amongst the people.

Jim

You shall eat here.

Tam-iTam

Time enough for eating later. We shall have to fight. The gates are closed.

Jim

Fight, what for?

Jewel

For our lives.

Jim

I have no life. Who knows? By audacity and cunning, we may even escape. There is much fear in men's hearts, too. Open the gates.

Tam-iTam

For how long, Tuan?

Jim

For all life.

Jewel

You must fight.

Jim

Time to finish this.

Tam-iTam

Tuan?

Jewel

Will you fight?

Jim

There is nothing to fight for, nothing is lost.

Jewel

Will you flee?

Jim

There is no escape.

Jewel

And shall you go?

(Jim bows his head.)

Jewel

You are mad or you are false. Do you remember the night I begged you to leave me and you said you could not? That it was impossible, impossible. Do you remember you said you would never leave me? Why? I asked you for no promise. You promised unasked. Remember?

Jim

Enough, girl. I should be worth having—

Jewel

For the last time, will you defend yourself?

Jim

No.

Jewel

I will hold you thus, you are mine.

(Jewel faints.)

Jim

Come here. Take her to the shelter.

Tam-iTam

Tuan. Tuan, look back.

(Jim signs and goes. Jewel recovers.)

Jewel (screaming)

You are false.

Jim

Forgive me.

Jewel

Never, never.

(The stage darkens and then we see Stein, Marlow, Jewel and Tam-iTam alone in Stein's palace.)

Tam-iTam

And that is the last we saw of him alive. He went to Doramin, alone, unarmed. Doramin was seated on his throne staring at his son's corpse which had been brought to him when Jim presented himself. Doramin rose slowly and shot him dead.

Jewel

He left me. You always leave us for your own ends. It would have been easy to die with him, but he would not let me. It was like blindness. And yet, it was I who stood before his eyes. It was me that he looked at all the time. You are hard, treacherous, without truth, without compassion. What makes you so wicked or is it that you are all bad? I will never forgive him. I will never cry for him.

Stein

Young hearts are unforgiving. The strength of life is in them. The cruel strength of life. Very frightful. She can't understand me. I am only a strange man. Perhaps you can make her see? Don't leave it like this. Tell her to forgive him.

Marlow

Have you forgiven him?

(The light fades and Marlow reappears with the guests on the verandah.)

And so, that is all. That is how he died. A romantic end. All or nearly all. For I met Brown one day a few years later. He was dying of fever in a Portuguese prison. I told him what happened.

(Brown appears suddenly, a dying man, against a background of bars.)

Brown

So, I paid that stuck-up beggar after all! I could see directly I set my eyes on him, what sort of a fool he was. He, a man! He was a hollow sham. Why couldn't he say straight out: "Hand off my plunder?" That would have been like a man. Damn him. Stuck-up bastard. He had me. But he didn't have the courage to make an end of me. Not he. Letting me off as if I wasn't worth a kick. Scorned by scum like him. He was just a fraud. So I did make an end to him after all. I expect this fever will kill me. But I shall die easier now. You may hear. I would give you a five pound note if I had it, for the news you've brought me or my name's not

Gentleman Brown.

(The light fades on Brown.)

Marlow

Brown was horrifying. He had a demon in him. He was one of those unconquerable spirits which, despite its evil, one cannot help wondering at. As for Jim, he is dead. And frankly, I'm angry with him. He gives up a living woman to celebrate a pitiless wedding with his shadowy ideal of honor. Is he satisfied now, I wonder? We ought to know, because he is one of us, isn't he?

A Guest

You are never satisfied, Marlow. Now you're angry with him because he gave up his life for an ideal which you can't quite see.

Marlow

In his place, I should not have given up my life for my position with those natives.

A Guest

Perhaps that's because you had a position somewhere else and he did not. But you condemn him for his cowardice in jumping off the boat and his heroism here?

Marlow

I take it that his heroism here was more the fear of losing face than real heroism.

A Guest

But don't you see how paradoxical your reasoning is? On the *Patna* you would have had Jim give up his life for no particular earthly good. He would have saved no lives, accomplished nothing. That you admit yourself. Was he wrong to jump?

Marlow

It was what happened before he jumped. It was what happened during the emergency.

A Guest

Perhaps so. But if he had stayed and the ship had gone down, what would he have been but a casualty? Who would have know his case but himself?

Marlow

But that was all important.

A Guest

I'm not so sure. I fully agree with what he did. The freezing was wrong, perhaps. But the jumping, no. If the ship was going down, as he thought, he had nothing else to do. But here you would have had him save his life?

Marlow

Yes. For that girl who was a real substantial woman. And for Stein and also for me. There was where his obligation lay.

A Guest

But did he not also have an obligation to the image he had created of himself? And to the world he had made? The civilization he had brought there? I think he did just as well to sacrifice himself then and not aboard the *Patna*. Perhaps it was for this destiny that his cowardice saved him in one instance to allow him a greater heroism and a more worthwhile death in another.

Marlow

I'm not sure I see it that way at all.

A Guest

Your position is to my mind rather mysterious. But that only proves what I've always believed, that the essence of all morality ends in a mystery.

Voices

He was a child.

He was false.

He was true.

I shall never weep for him.

(Sobbing is heard.)

CURTAIN

ABOUT THE AUTHOR

Frank J. Morlock has written and translated many plays since retiring from the legal profession in 1992. His translations have also appeared on Project Gutenberg, the Alexandre Dumas Père web page, Literature in the Age of Napoléon, Infinite Artistries.com, and Munsey's (formerly Blackmask). In 2006 he received an award from the North American Jules Verne Society for his translations of Verne's plays. He lives and works in México.

www.ingramcontent.com/pod-product-compliance
Lightning Source LLC
LaVergne TN
LVHW041628070426
835507LV00008B/504